PIANO · VOCAL · GUITAR

THIRD DAY
LEAD US BACK   SONGS OF WORSHIP

ISBN 978-1-4950-1905-0

HAL•LEONARD® CORPORATION
7777 W. BLUEMOUND RD. P.O. BOX 13819 MILWAUKEE, WI 53213

Visit Hal Leonard Online at
www.halleonard.com

SPIRIT

Words and Music by MAC POWELL,
TAI ANDERSON, MARK LEE,
DAVID CARR and JUSTIN DALY

Moderate Ballad

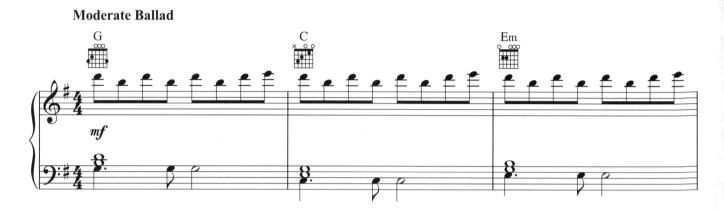

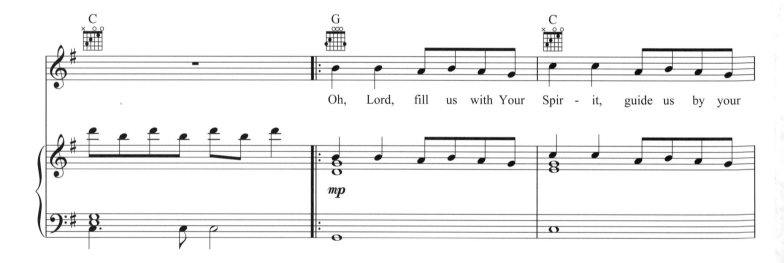

Oh, Lord, fill us with Your Spir - it, guide us by your

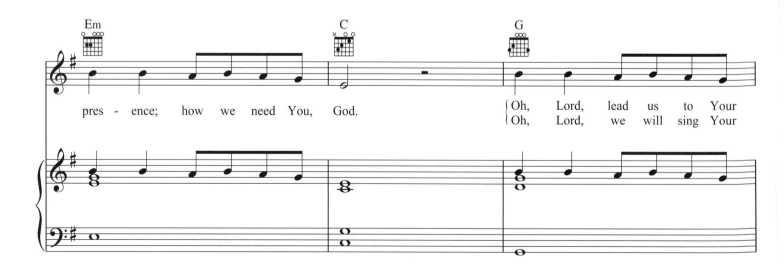

pres - ence; how we need You, God.

Oh, Lord, lead us to Your
Oh, Lord, we will sing Your

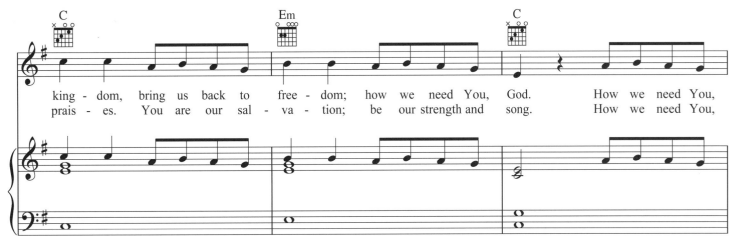

king - dom, bring us back to free - dom; how we need You, God. How we need You,
prais - es. You are our sal - va - tion; be our strength and song. How we need You,

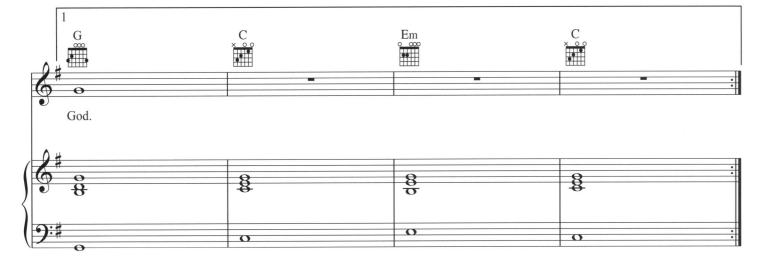

God.

God. How we need You, God.

How we need You, God. How we need You,

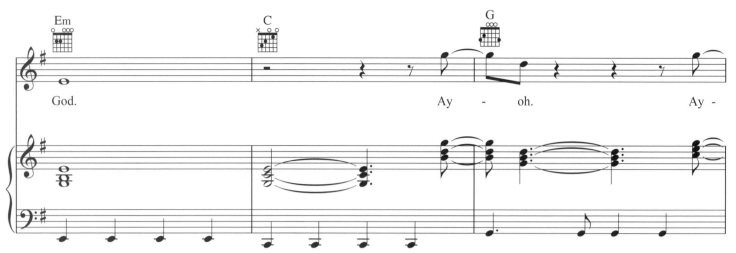

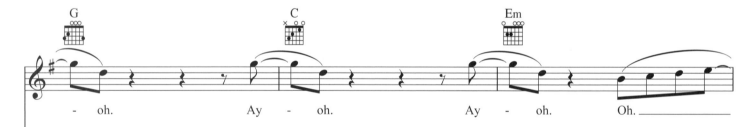

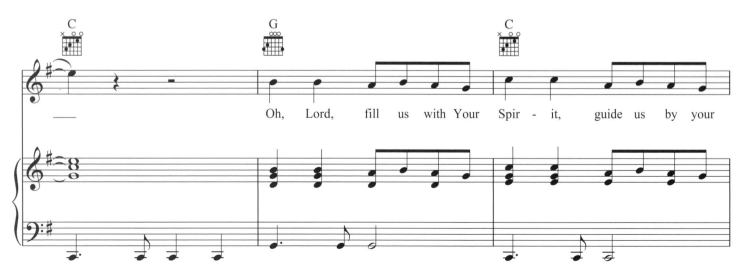

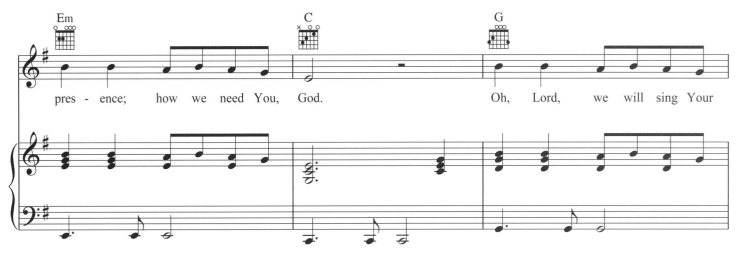

pres - ence; how we need You, God.   Oh, Lord,   we will sing Your

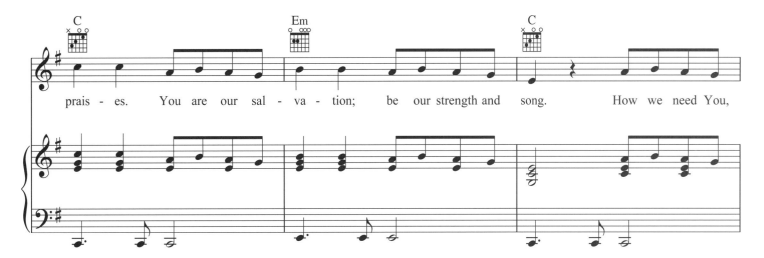

prais - es.   You are our sal - va - tion; be our strength and song.   How we need You,

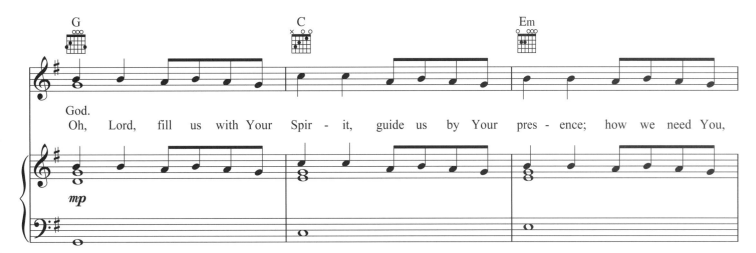

God.
Oh, Lord, fill us with Your Spir - it, guide us by Your pres - ence; how we need You,

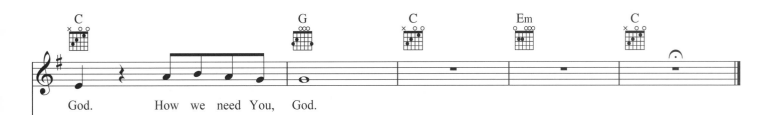

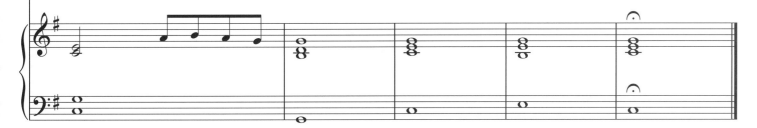

God.   How we need You, God.

SOUL ON FIRE

Words and Music by BRENTON BROWN,
MAC POWELL, TAI ANDERSON, MARK LEE,
DAVID CARR and MATT MAHER

Southern Rock

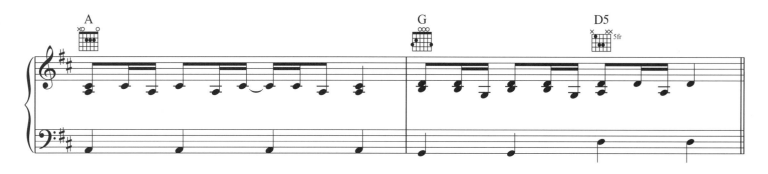

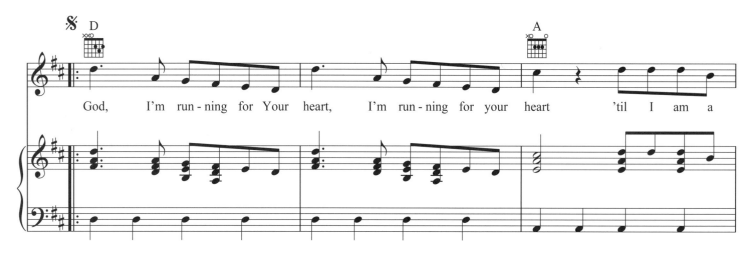

God, I'm run-ning for Your heart, I'm run-ning for your heart 'til I am a

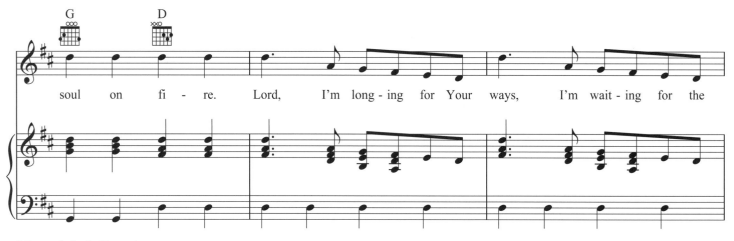

soul on fi-re. Lord, I'm long-ing for Your ways, I'm wait-ing for the

* *Recorded a half step lower.*

To Coda ⊕

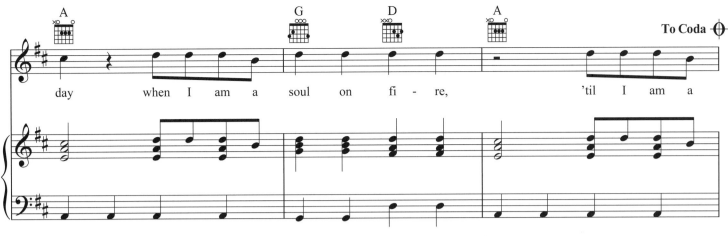

day when I am a soul on fi - re, 'til I am a

1.

soul on fi - re.

2.

soul on fi - re.

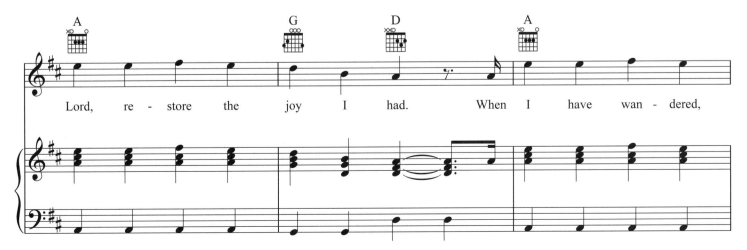

Lord, re - store the joy I had. When I have wan - dered,

8

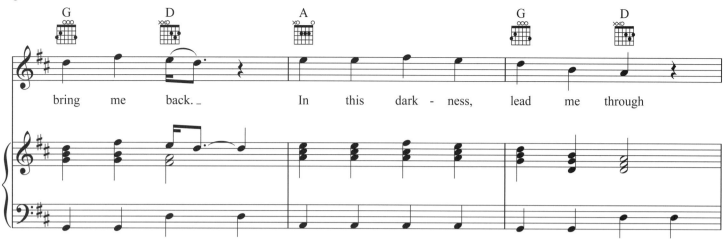

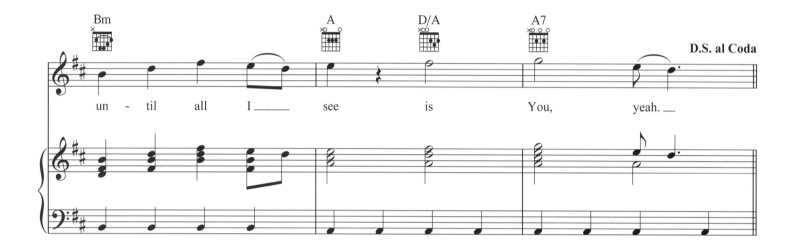

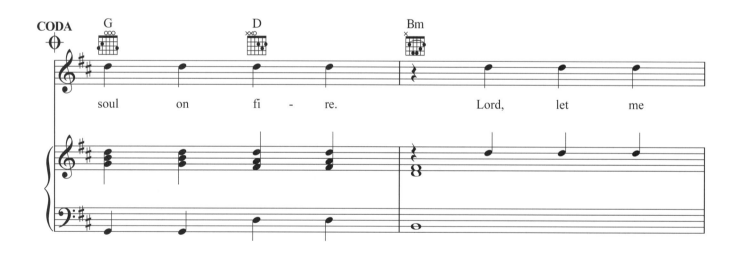

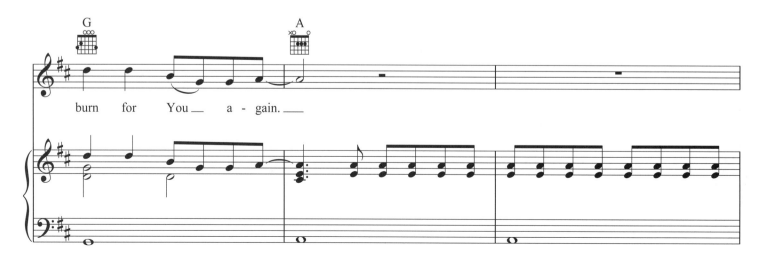

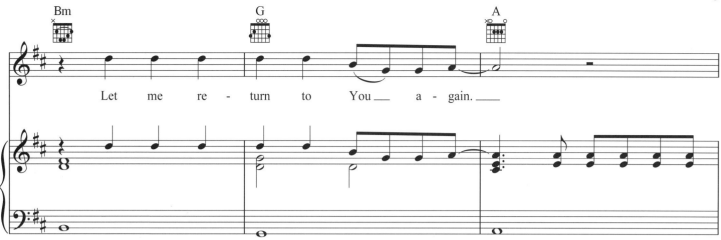

Let me re- turn to You __ a- gain. __

Lord, let me burn for You __ a - gain. __

Let me re-

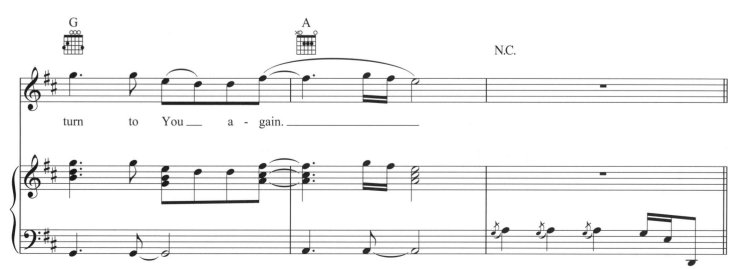

turn to You __ a - gain. __

God, I'm run-ning for Your heart, I'm run-ning for Your heart 'til I am a
Lord, I'm long-ing for Your ways, I'm wait-ing for the day when I am a
God, I'm run-ning for Your heart, I'm run-ning for Your heart 'til I am a

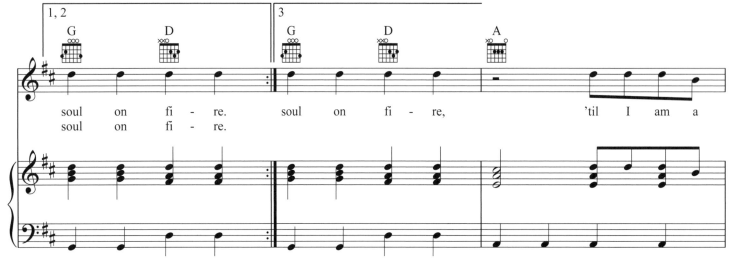

soul on fi-re. soul on fi-re, 'til I am a
soul on fi-re.

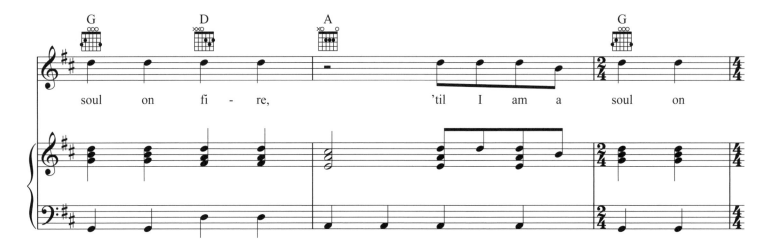

soul on fi-re, 'til I am a soul on

fi - re.

YOUR WORDS

Words and Music by MAC POWELL,
TAI ANDERSON, MARK LEE and DAVID CARR

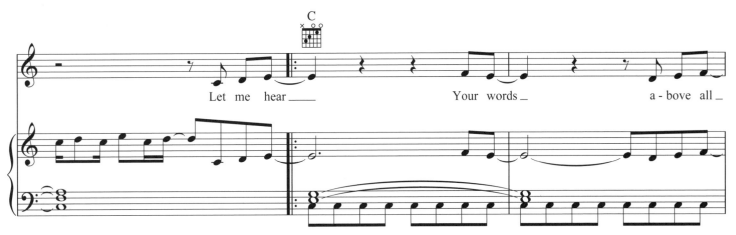

Let me hear ___ Your words ___ a-bove all ___

___ oth-er voic ___ -es, ___ a-bove all ___ the dis-trac-

- tions in ___ this world. ___ Let me hear ___

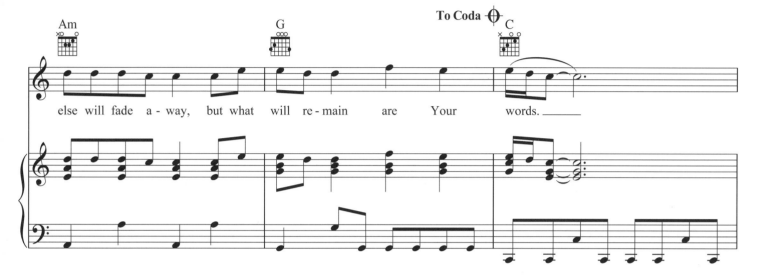

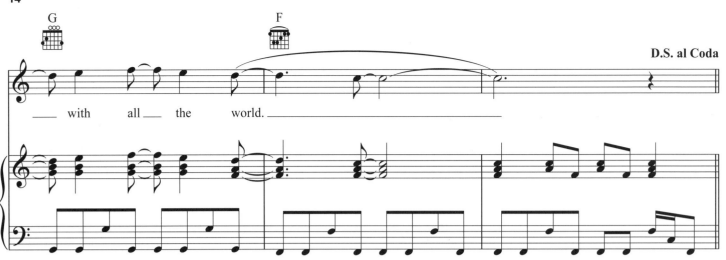

D.S. al Coda

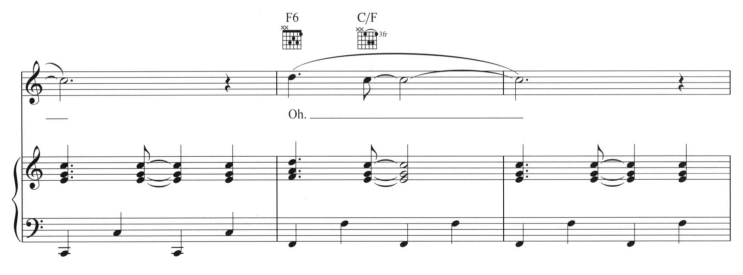

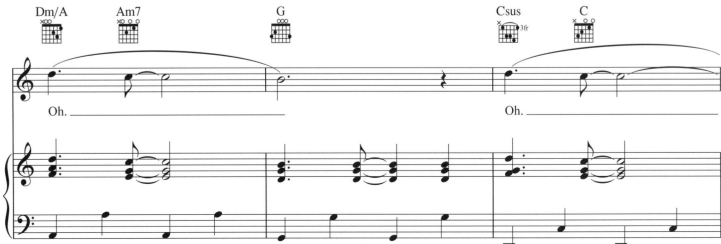

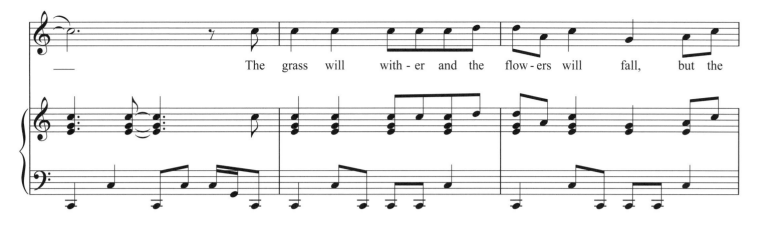

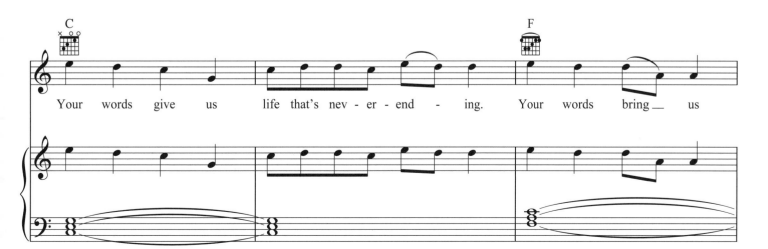

love that nev- er fails. Ev-'ry-thing else will fade a- way, but what will re- main are Your

Your words give us life that's nev - er - end - ing. Your words bring_ us
words.

love that nev- er fails. Ev-'ry-thing else will fade a- way, but what will re- main are Your_

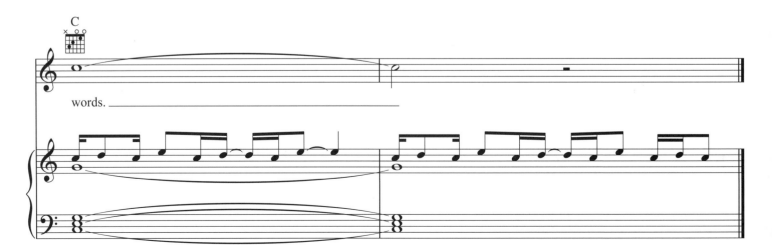

words. _____

OUR DELIVERER

Words and Music by MAC POWELL,
TAI ANDERSON, MARK LEE,
DAVID CARR and JUSTIN DALY

With a solid backbeat

There is beau-ty ___ a-ris-ing from these ash-es. There is new life
Ev-'ry bur-den ___ one day will be lift-ed. Ev-'ry bro-ken

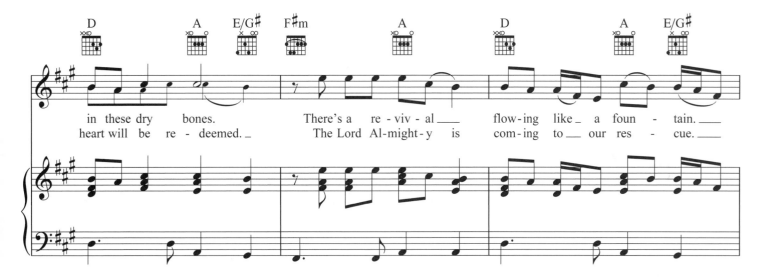

in these dry bones. There's a re-viv-al ___ flow-ing like ___ a foun-tain. ___
heart will be re-deemed. ___ The Lord Al-might-y is com-ing to ___ our res-cue. ___

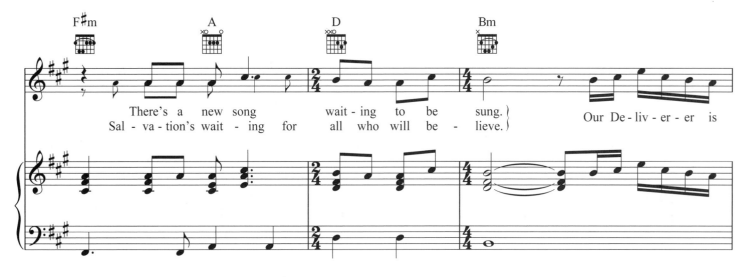

There's a new song wait-ing to be sung.
Sal-va-tion's wait-ing for all who will be-lieve.

Our De-liv-er-er is

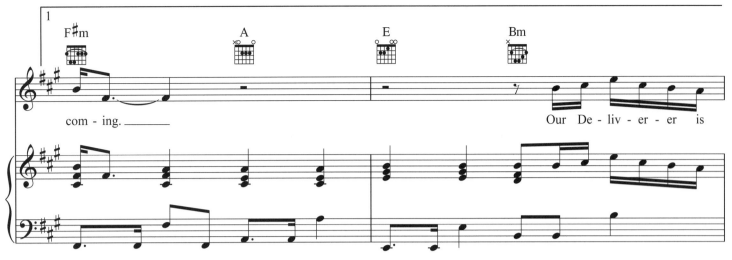

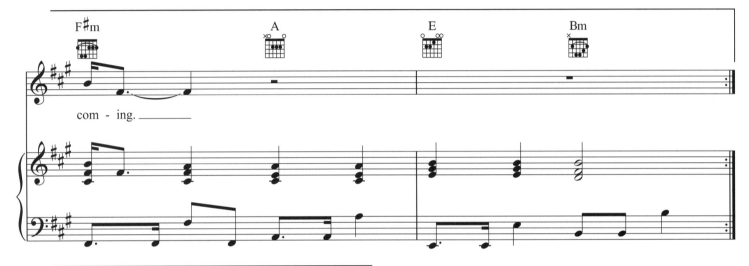

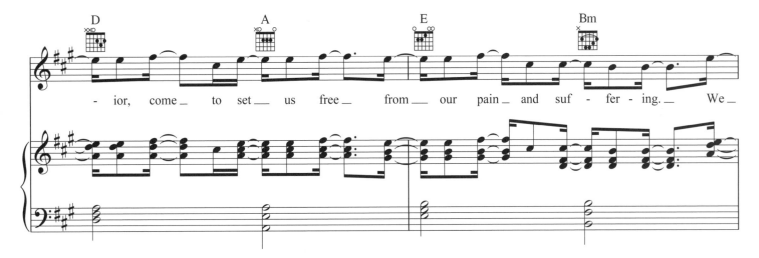

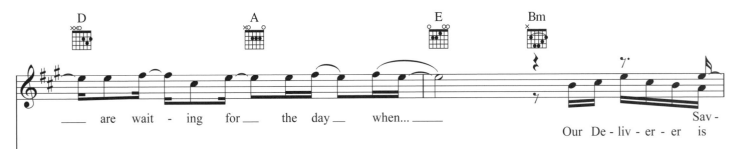

com-ing _____ with _ sal - va - tion in _ His wings. _ Our De - liv - er - er is

com-ing, _____ here _ to set _____ His peo - ple free. _ Our De - liv - er - er. _

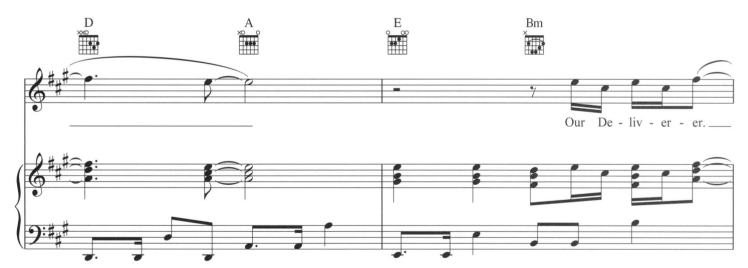

_____ Our De - liv - er - er. _

_____ Sav -

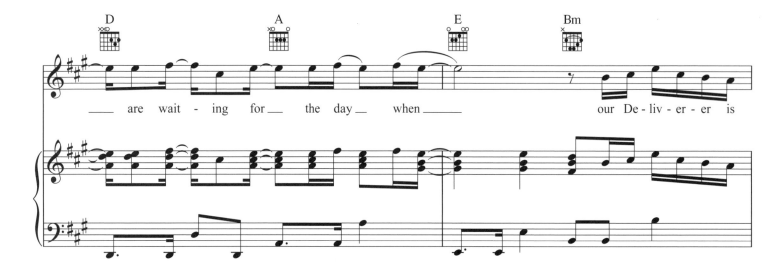

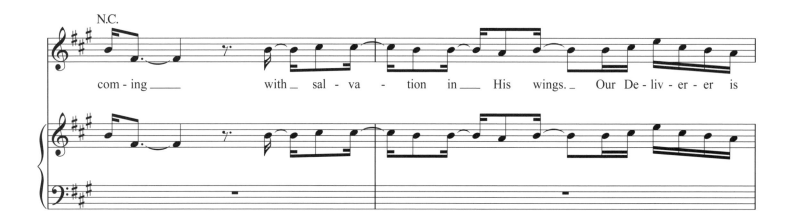

HE IS ALIVE

Words and Music by MAC POWELL,
TAI ANDERSON, MARK LEE and DAVID CARR

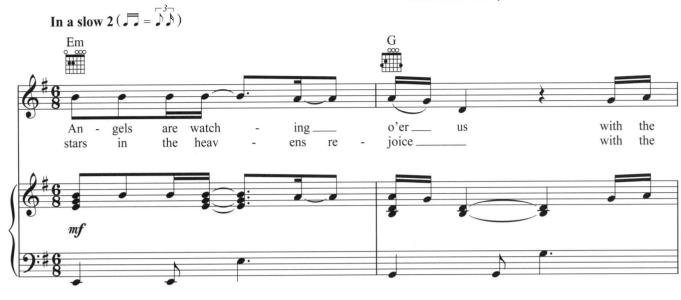

An - gels are watch - ing ___ o'er ___ us with the
stars in the heav - ens re - joice ___ with the

saints that have gone ___ on be - fore ___ us. ___ And they
sun and the moon ___ and with all ___ of the ___ earth. ___ Let

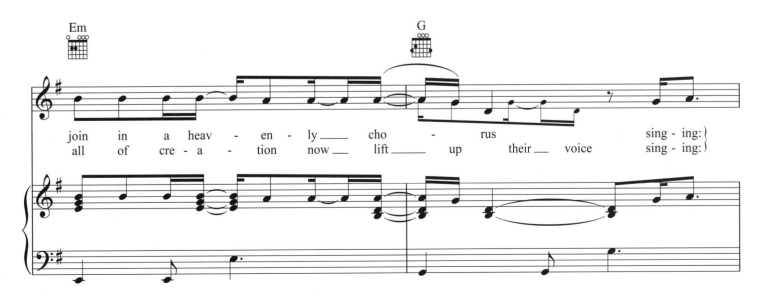

join in a heav - en - ly ___ cho - rus sing - ing:
all of cre - a - tion now ___ lift ___ up their ___ voice sing - ing:

He is a-live,__ He is a-live.__ He is a-live;__

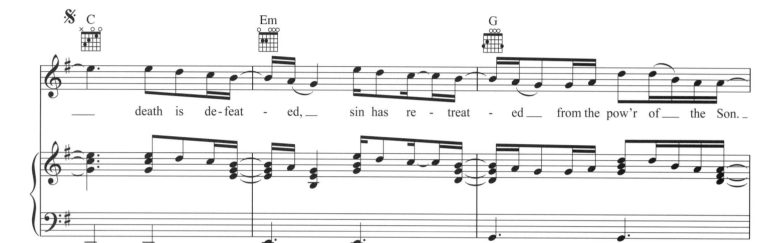

__ death is de-feat -ed,__ sin has re -treat -ed__ from the pow'r of __ the Son.__

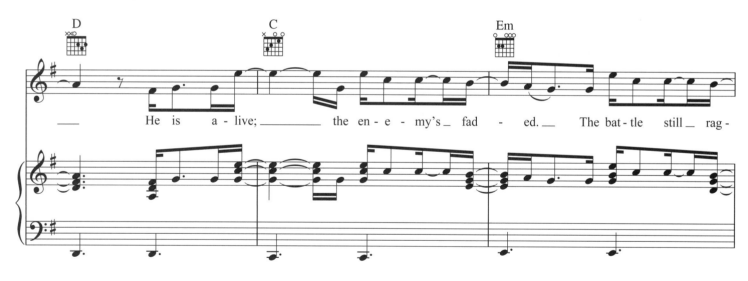

__ He is a -live;__ the en -e -my's__ fad -ed.__ The bat -tle still__ rag-

-es,__ but the war has been won.__ The __ Je -sus is __ a-

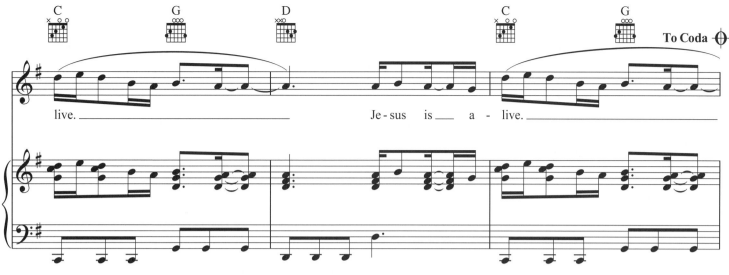

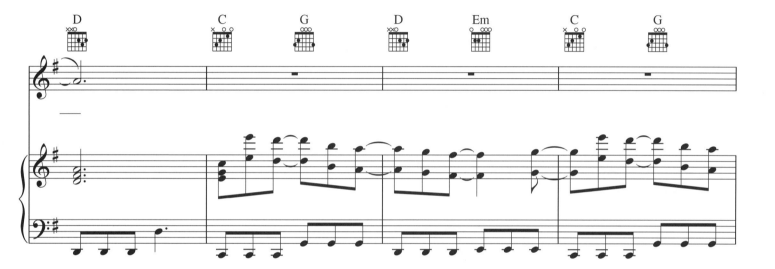

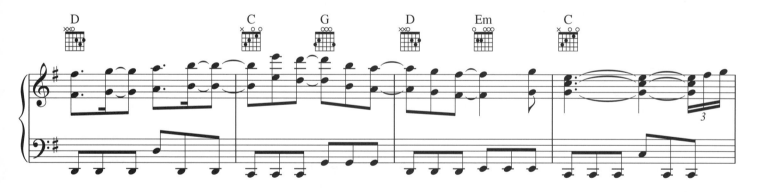

live. ___ Je-sus is ___ a-live. ___

He is a - live; ___ death is de-feat - ed, ___ sin has re-treat-

26

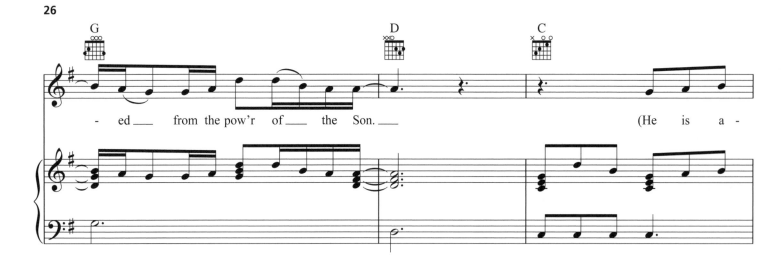

-ed___ from the pow'r of ___ the Son. ___ (He is a-

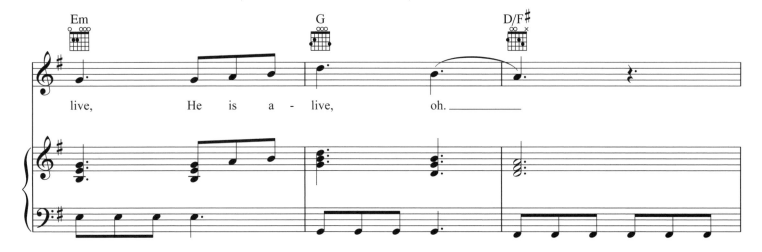

live, He is a - live, oh. ___

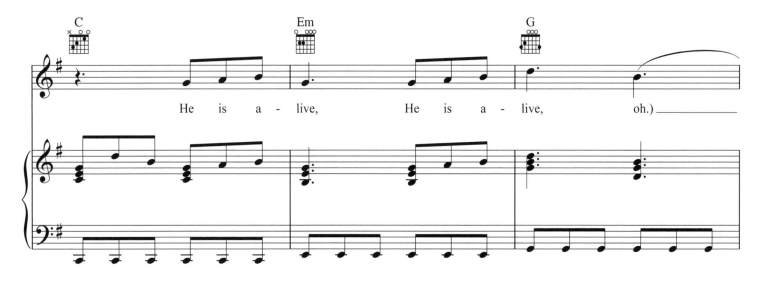

He is a - live, He is a - live, oh.) ___

D.S. al Coda
(take 2nd ending)

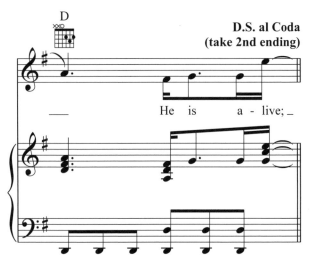

He is a - live; _

CODA

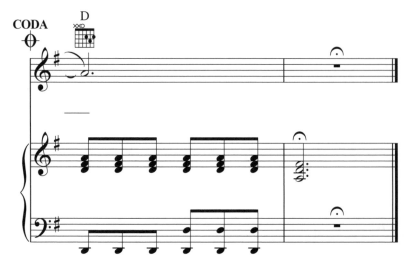

IN JESUS NAME

Words and Music by MAC POWELL,
TAI ANDERSON, MARK LEE and DAVID CARR

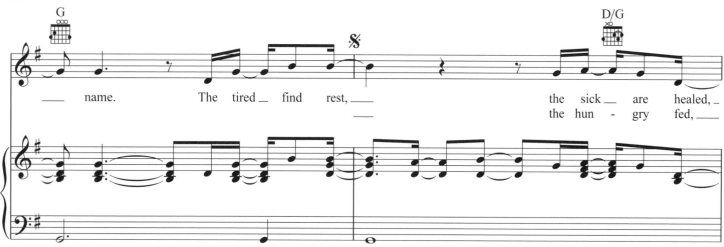

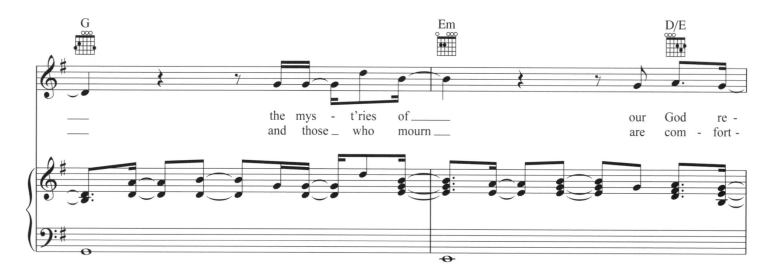

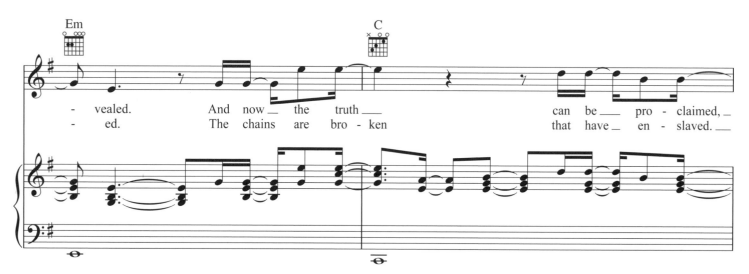

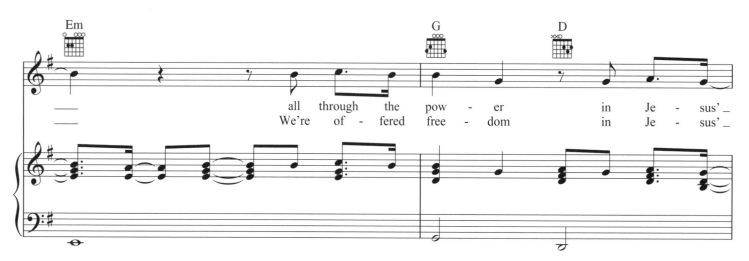

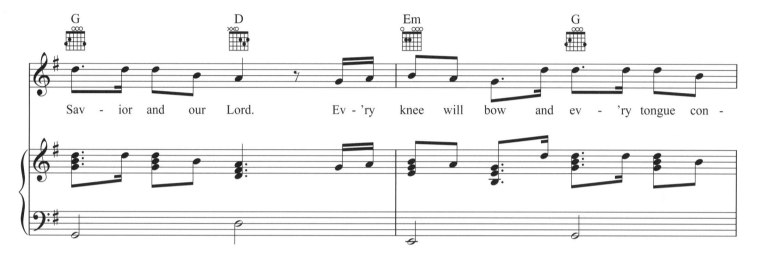

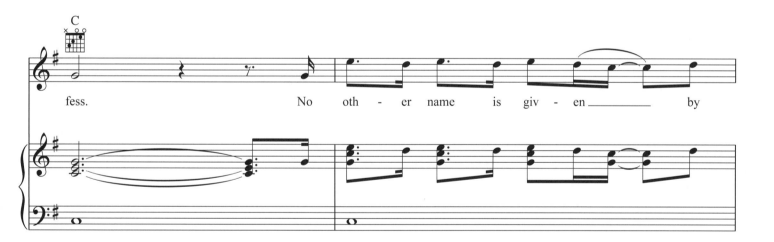

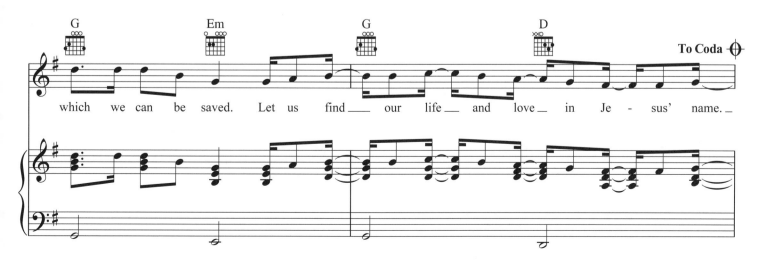

D.S. al Coda

The thirst - y filled, __

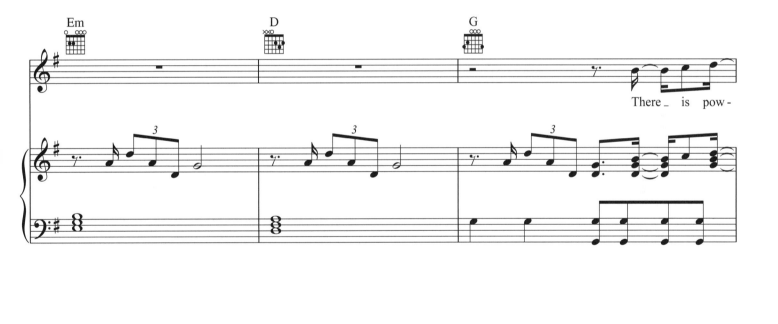

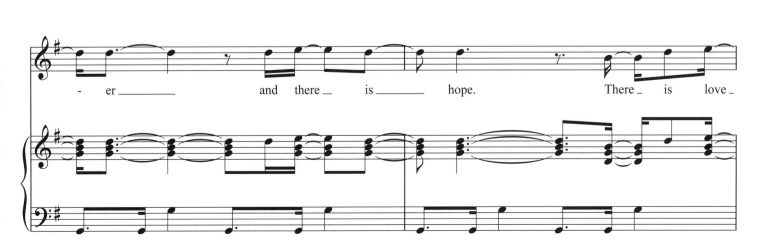

like you've nev - er known. _____ There is _____ for - give-

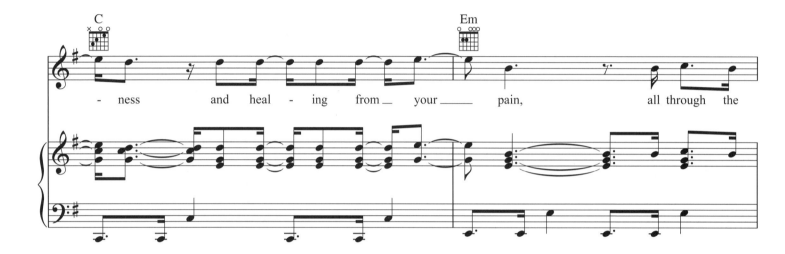

- ness _____ and heal - ing from _____ your _____ pain, _____ all through the

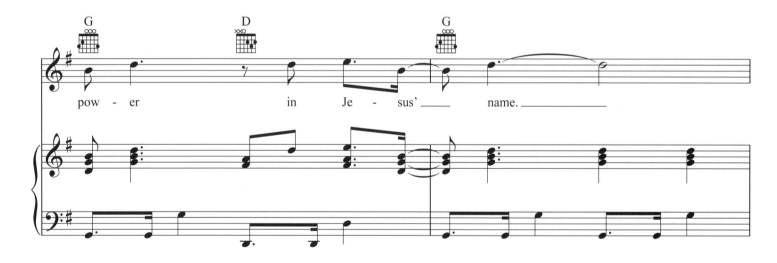

pow - er _____ in Je - sus' _____ name. _____

Name a - bove all ___ names, _____ Sav - ior and our Lord. Ev - 'ry

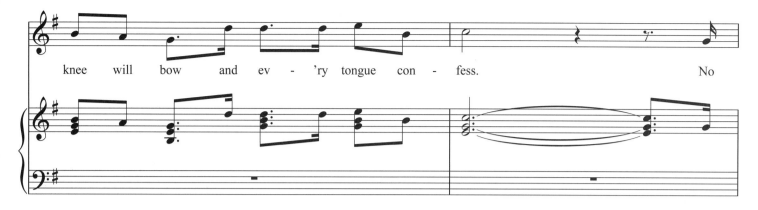

knee will bow and ev - 'ry tongue con - fess. No

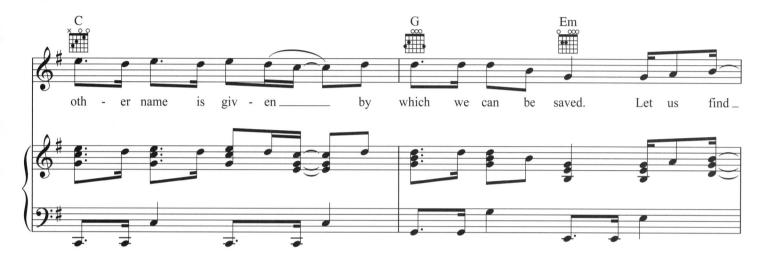

oth - er name is giv - en ___ by which we can be saved. Let us find _

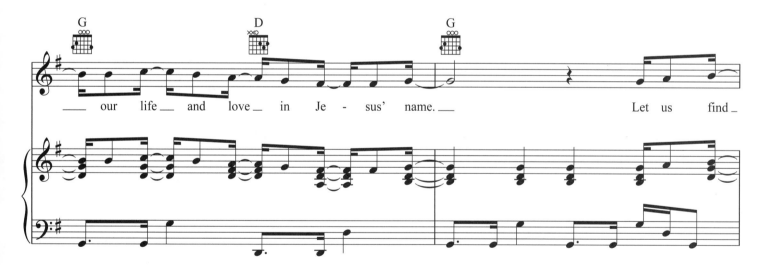

___ our life _ and love _ in Je - sus' name. ___ Let us find _

___ our life ___ and love ___ in Je - sus' name.

LEAD US BACK

Words and Music by MAC POWELL,
TAI ANDERSON, MARK LEE and DAVID CARR

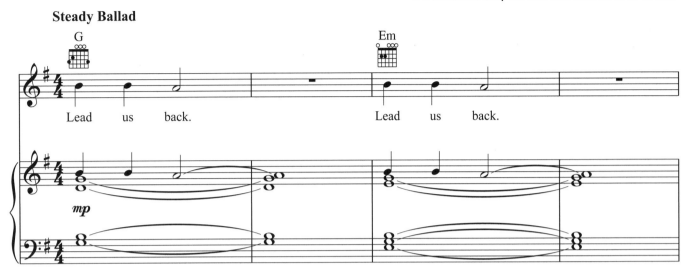

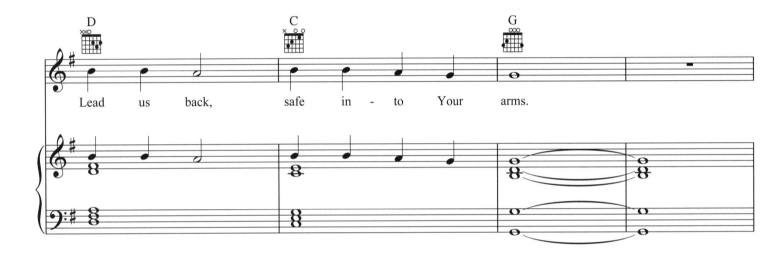

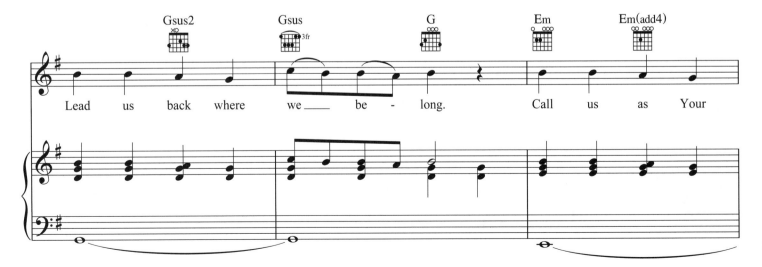

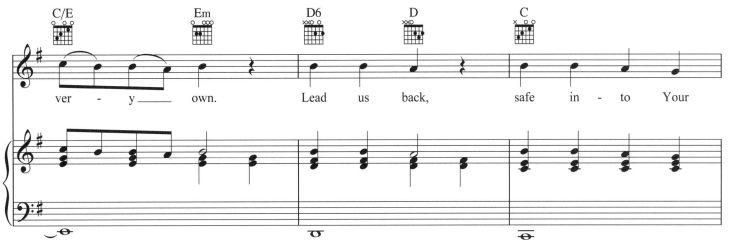

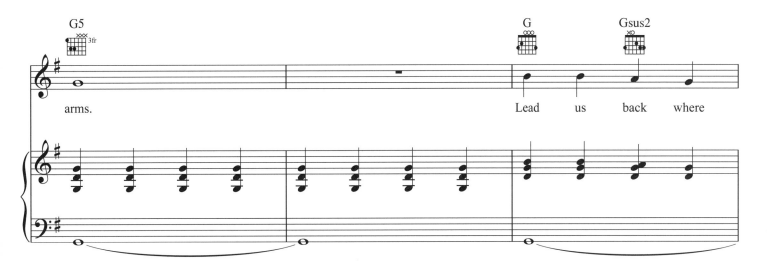

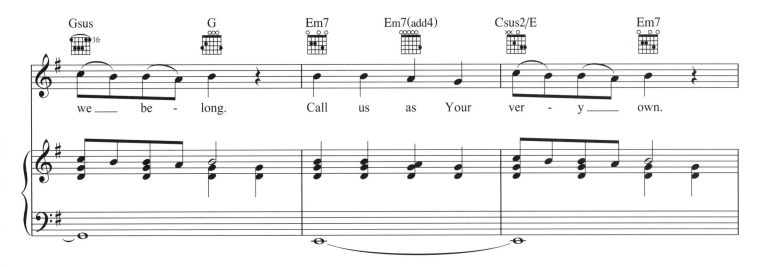

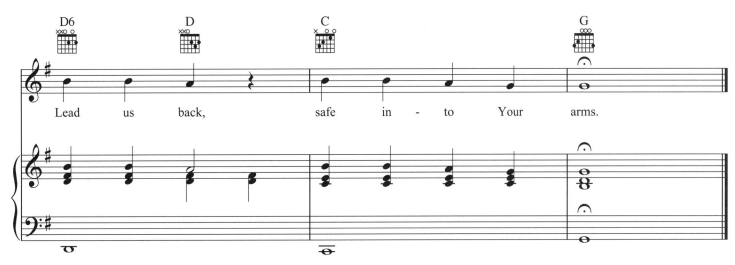

MAKER

Words and Music by MAC POWELL,
TAI ANDERSON, MARK LEE and DAVID CARR

Moderately fast

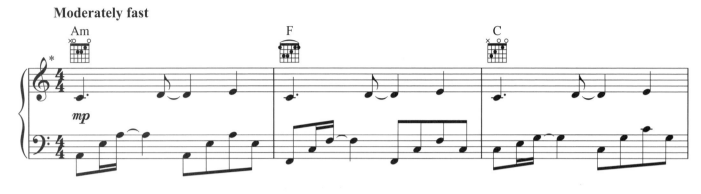

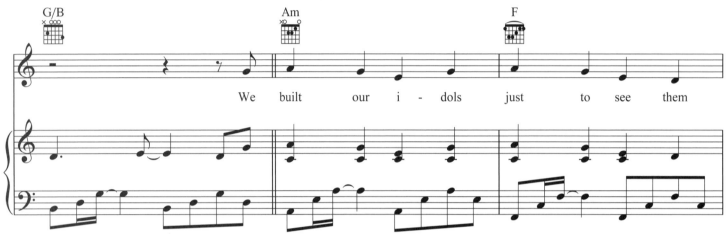

We built our i - dols just to see them

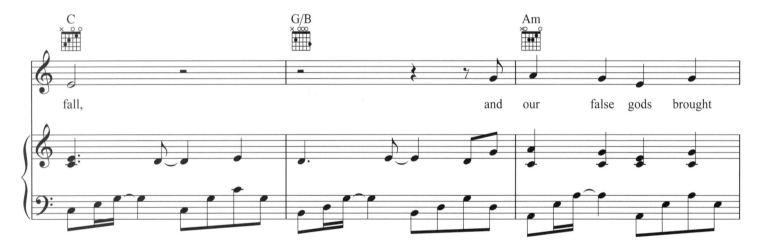

fall, and our false gods brought

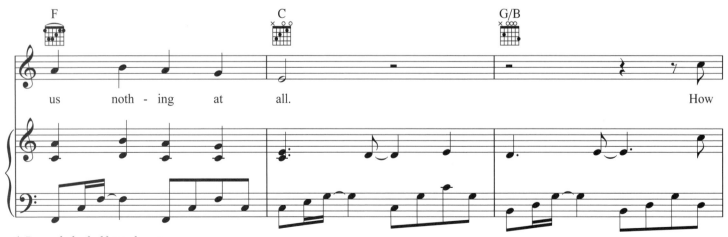

us noth - ing at all. How

* Recorded a half step lower.

foolish we ___ have been; for- give us for ___ our ___

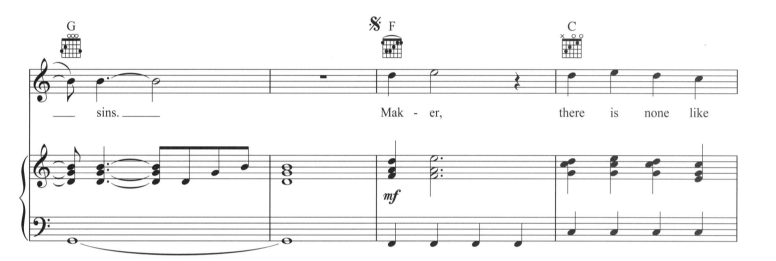

___ sins. ___ Mak - er, there is none like

You. Sav - ior, no one else will

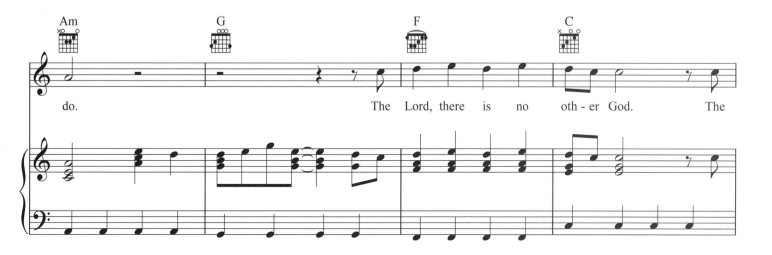

do. The Lord, there is no oth - er God. The

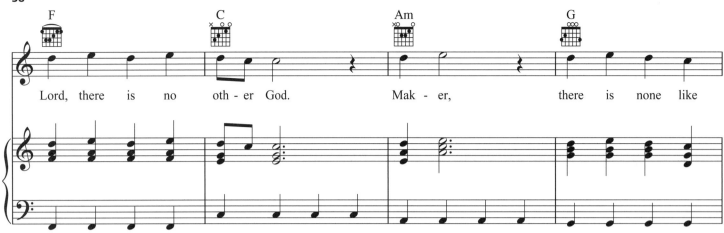

Lord, there is no oth-er God. Mak- er, there is none like

You. And on our own, we have noth-ing but

shame. But by Your grace, we all can stand a-

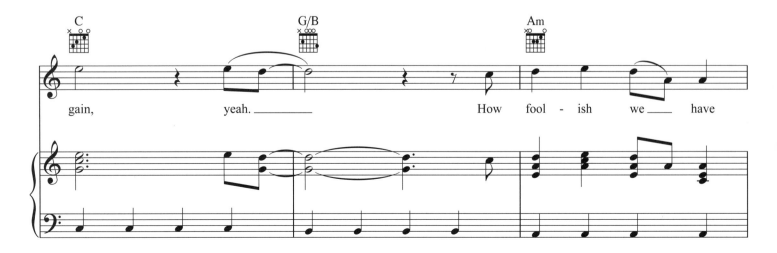

gain, yeah._____ How fool - ish we ___ have

D.S. al Coda

been; for-give us for __ our __ sins. __

CODA

Gath-er __ to-geth-er, all a-round __ the world.

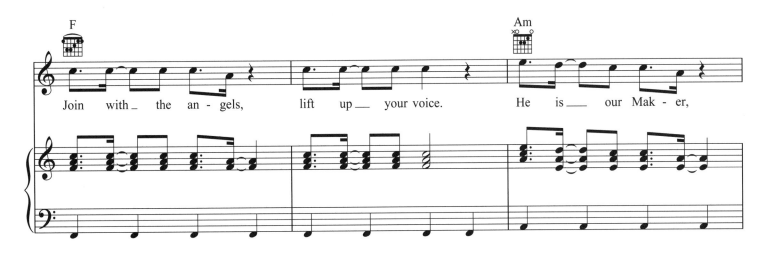

Join with __ the an-gels, lift up __ your voice. He is __ our Mak-er,

He is __ our God and __ our __ Lord. __

Gath - er to - geth - er all a - round the world. Join with the an - gels,

lift up your voice. He is our Mak - er, He is our God and our

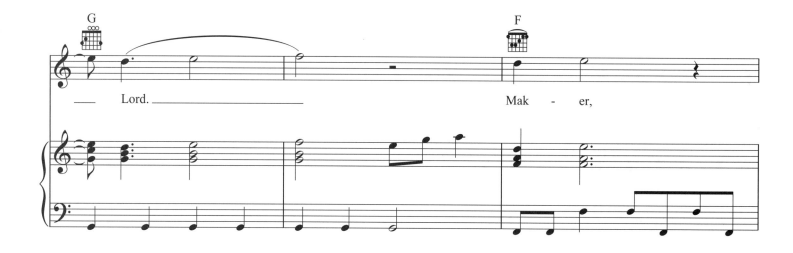

Lord. Mak - er,

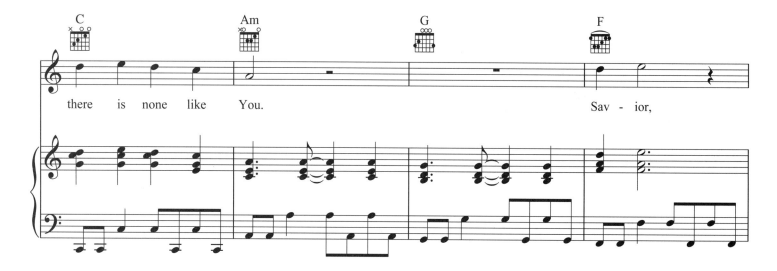

there is none like You. Sav - ior,

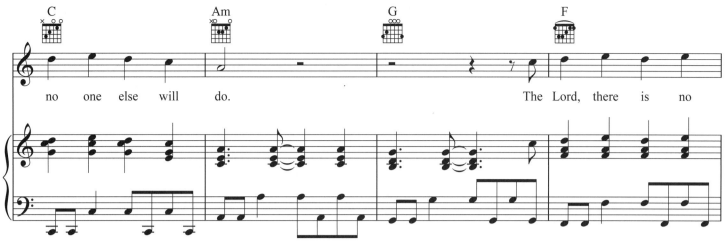

no one else will do. The Lord, there is no

oth-er God. The Lord, there is no oth-er God. Mak - er,

there is none like You. Our

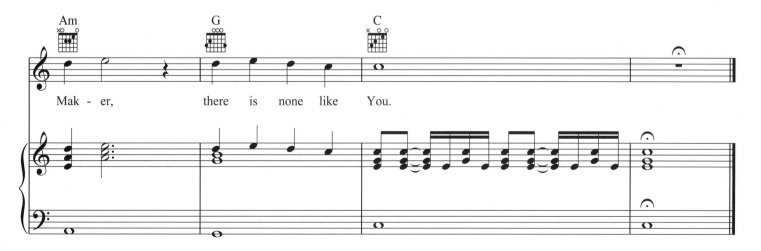

Mak - er, there is none like You.

VICTORIOUS

Words and Music by MAC POWELL,
TAI ANDERSON, MARK LEE,
DAVID CARR and JUSTIN DALY

Moderately

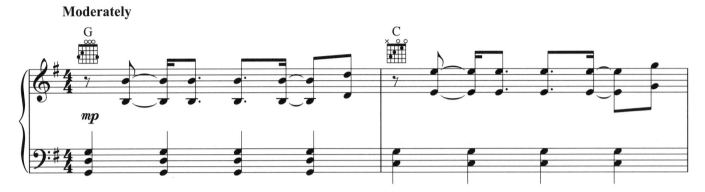

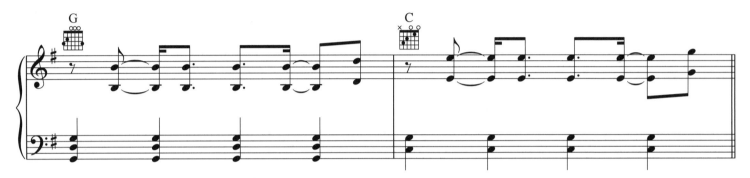

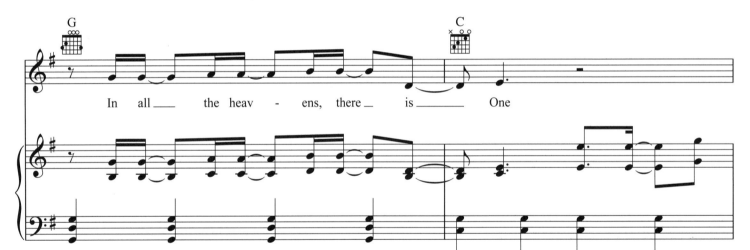

In all ___ the heav - ens, there ___ is ___ One

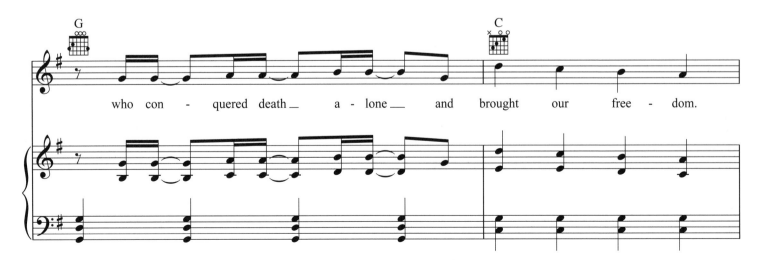

who con - quered death ___ a - lone ___ and brought our free - dom.

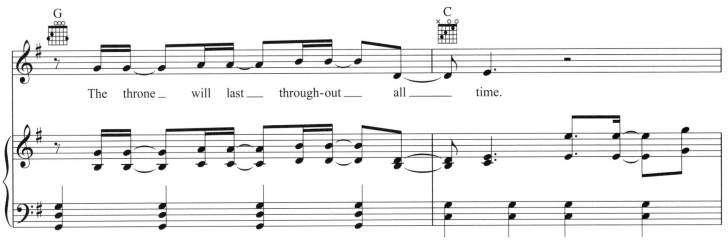

The throne __ will last __ through-out __ all _____ time.

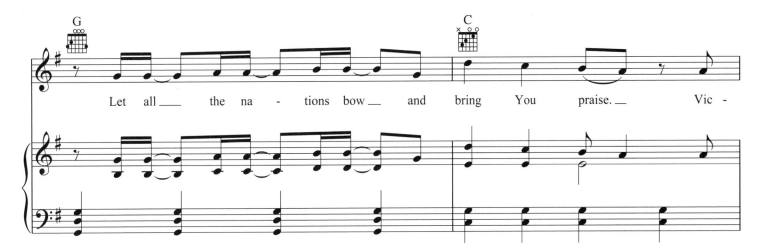

Let all __ the na - tions bow __ and bring You praise. __ Vic -

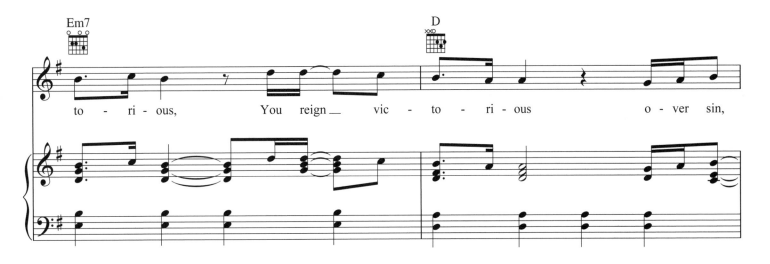

to - ri - ous, You reign __ vic - to - ri - ous over sin,

o - ver death, o - ver all, o - ver us. _____

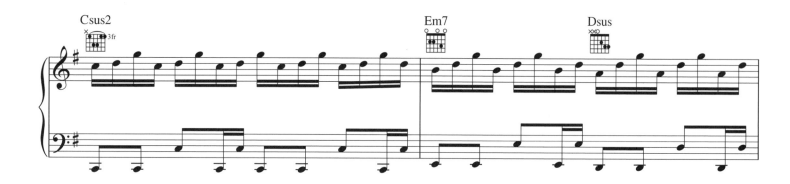

And with _ the an - gels we _ will _

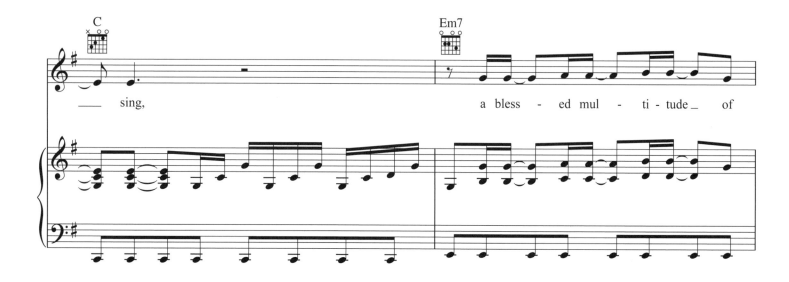

_ sing,   a bless - ed mul - ti - tude _ of

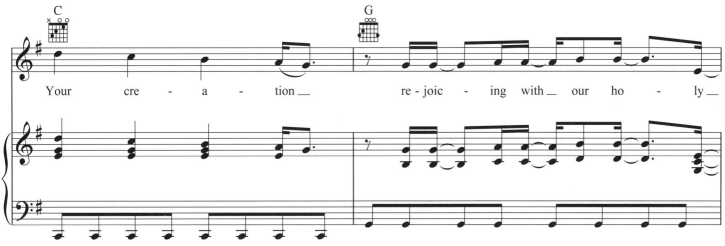

Your cre - a - tion _ re - joic - ing with _ our ho - ly _

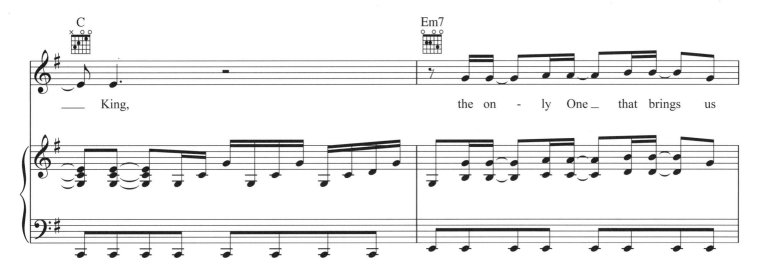

_ King, the on - ly One _ that brings us

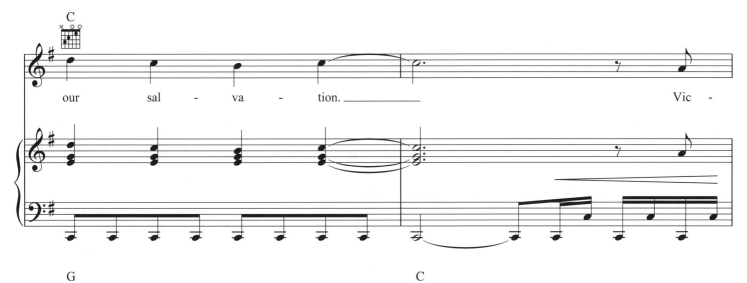

our sal - va - tion. _ Vic -

to - ri - ous, You reign _ vic - to - ri - ous o - ver sin,

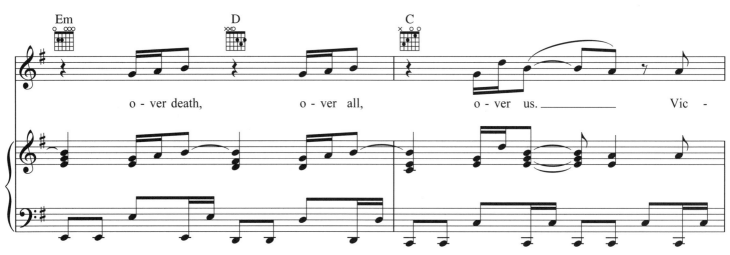

o - ver death, o - ver all, o - ver us. _____ Vic -

to - ri - ous, You reign_ vic - to - ri - ous. In Your might -

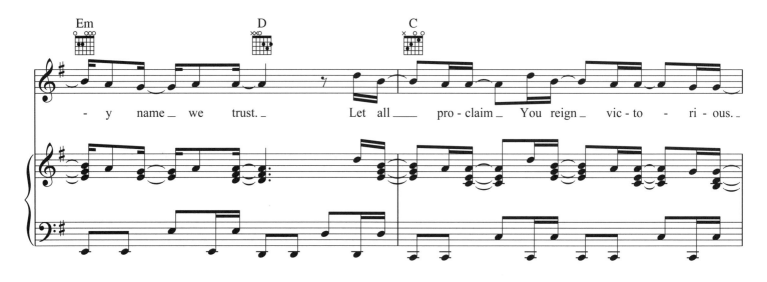

- y name_ we trust._ Let all___ pro - claim_ You reign_ vic - to - ri - ous.

___ (Vic - to - ri - ous, _____ we lift You up, ____

vic - to - ri - ous.) _____

All na - tions rise and they will ___ fall; _____

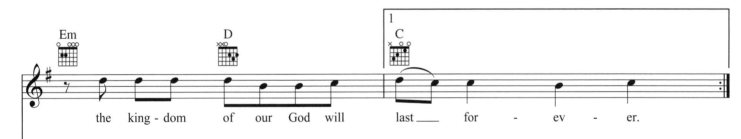

the king - dom of our God will last ___ for - ev - er.

last ___ for - ev - er. ___ (Vic - to - ri - ous, ___

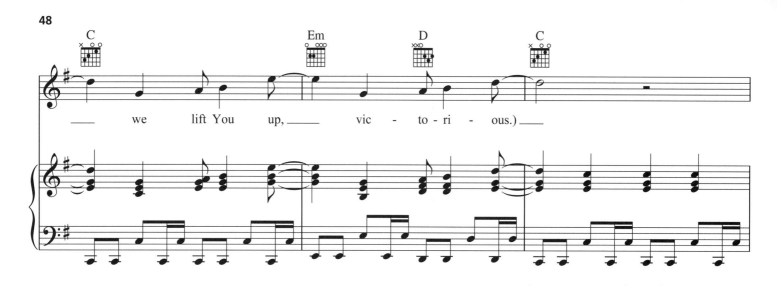

we lift You up, _____ vic - to - ri - ous.) _____

(Vic - to - ri - ous, _____ we lift You up, _____ vic - to - ri - ous.) _____

Vic - to - ri - ous, You reign _ vic - to - ri - ous _ o - ver sin,

o - ver death, o - ver all, o - ver us. _____

I KNOW YOU CAN

Words and Music by MAC POWELL,
TAI ANDERSON, MARK LEE and DAVID CARR

Moderately fast

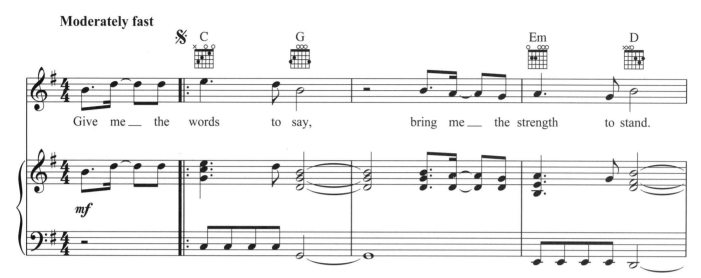

Give me the words to say, bring me the strength to stand.

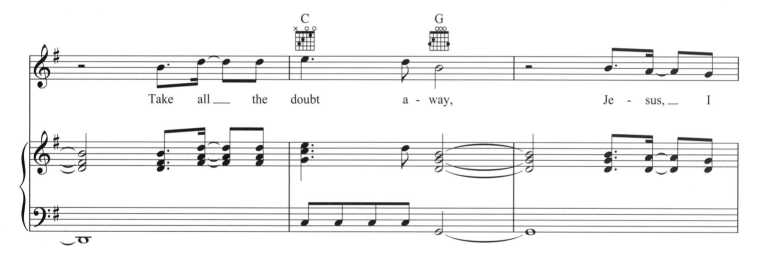

Take all the doubt a-way, Je-sus, I

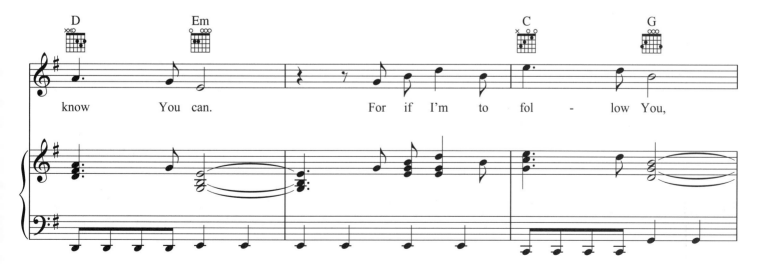

know You can. For if I'm to fol-low You,

it's on - ly by Your hand.   Help me ___ to make   it through,

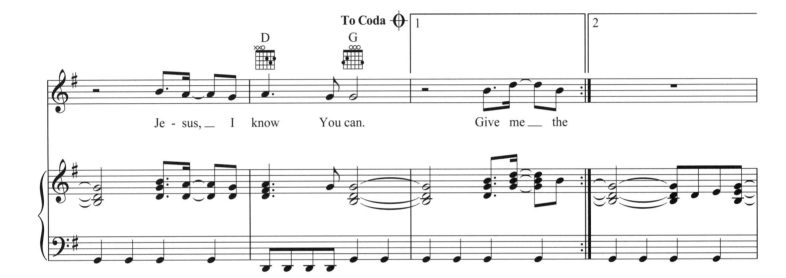

Je - sus, ___ I know   You can.   Give me ___ the

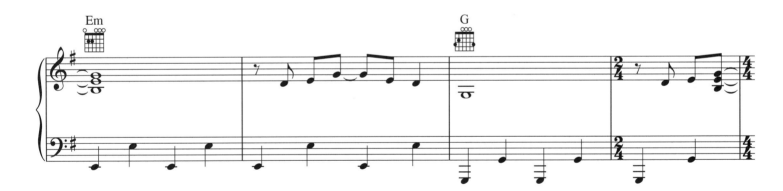

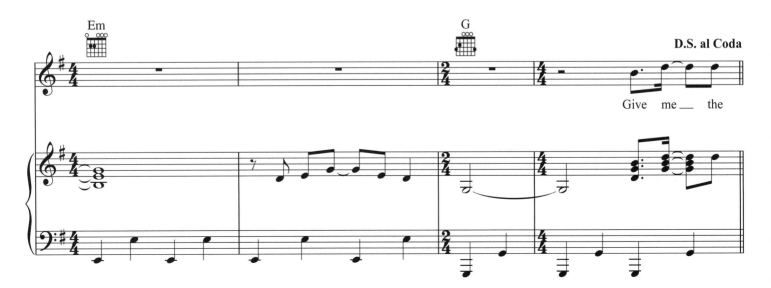

Give me ___ the

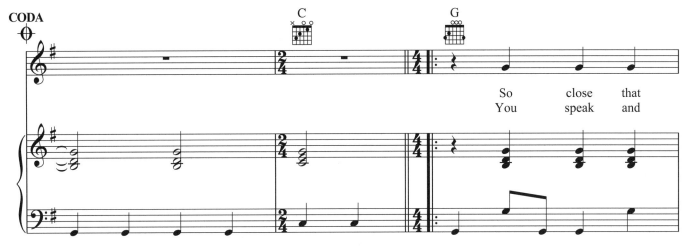

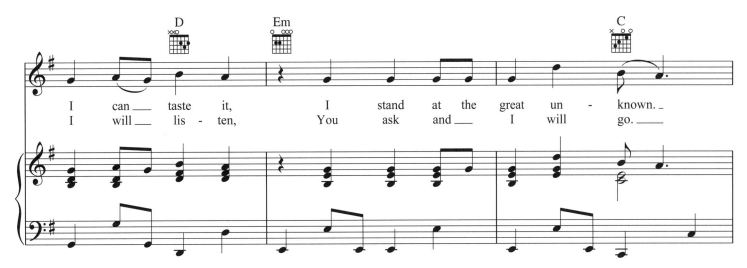

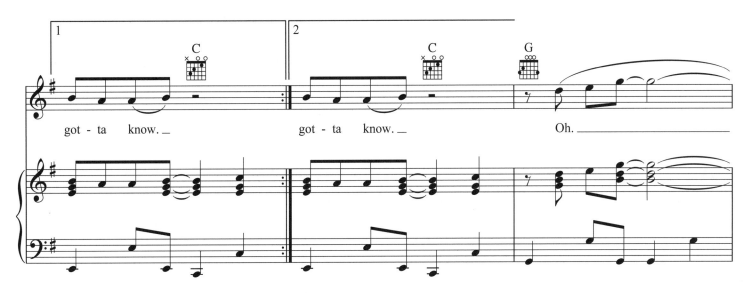

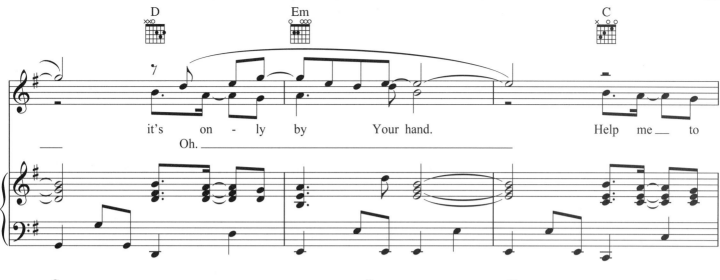

it's on - ly by Your hand.
Oh. _____

Help me to

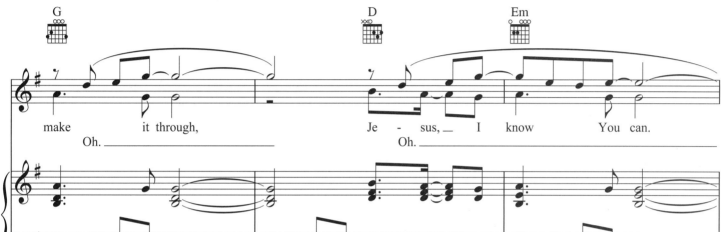

make it through,
Oh. _____

Je - sus, _ I know You can.
Oh. _____

Oh. _____

Oh. _____

Repeat and Fade | **Optional Ending**

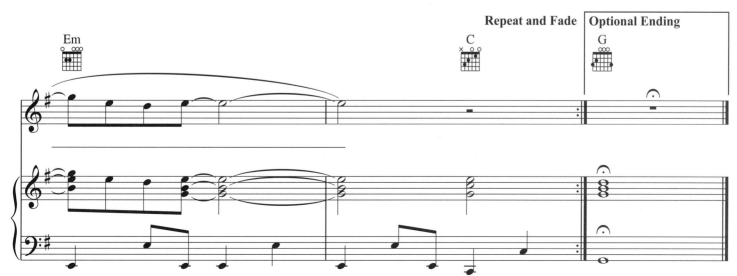

FATHER OF LIGHTS

Words and Music by MAC POWELL,
TAI ANDERSON, MARK LEE and DAVID CARR

With energy

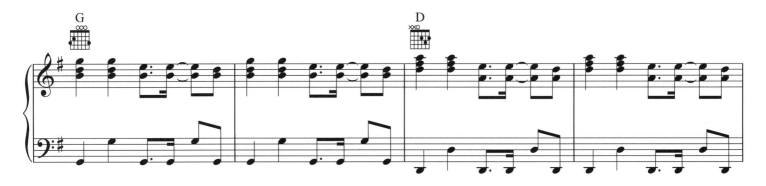

Fa - ther of love, Fa - ther

of lights,   let __

Your love fall, let it shine bright. _____

C

You ___ a - lone ___ de - serve the hon - or and the glo - ry, You ___

G   D

___ a - lone ___ de - serve all our praise, so ___ we wor - ship You ___

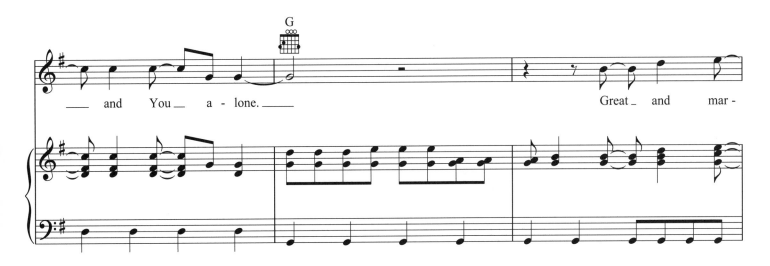

G

___ and You ___ a - lone. ___   Great ___ and mar -

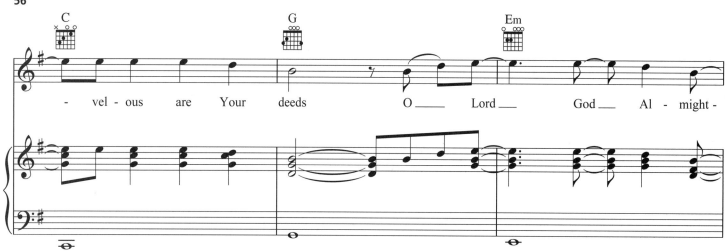

-vel-ous are Your deeds O___ Lord___ God___ Al-might-

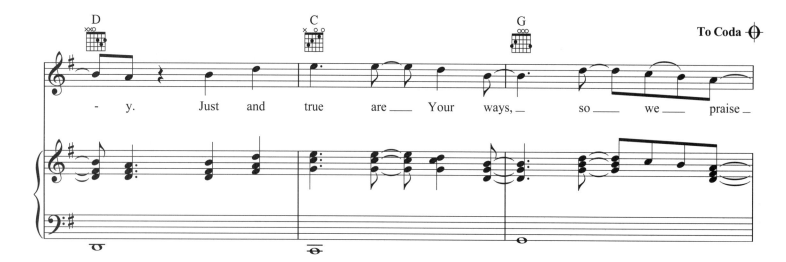

-y. Just and true are ___ Your ways, ___ so ___ we ___ praise ___

To Coda ⊕

___ You ___ and You ___ a-lone. ___

Fa - ther of truth, Fa - ther of grace,

be ____ with us now through

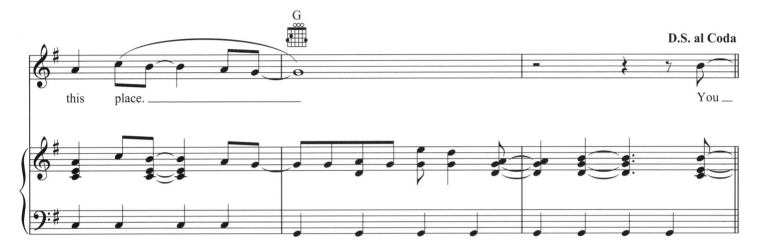

D.S. al Coda

this place. _____ You __

CODA

Great __ and mar - vel - ous are Your

deeds, O ____ Lord ____ God __ Al - might - y. Just and

58

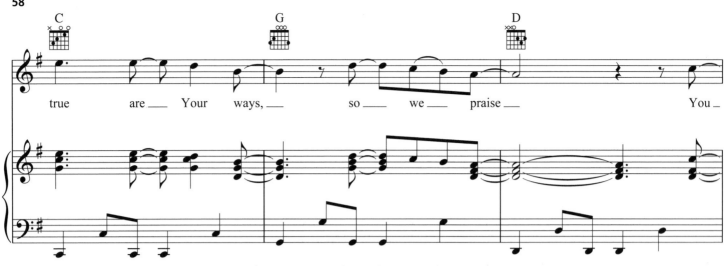

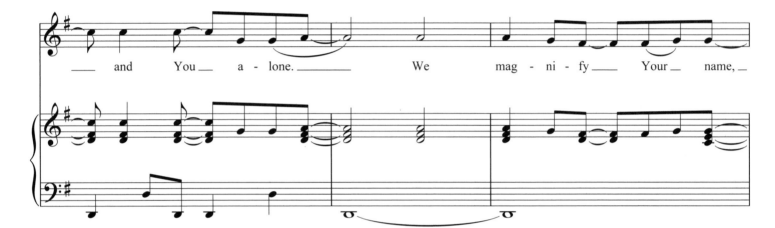

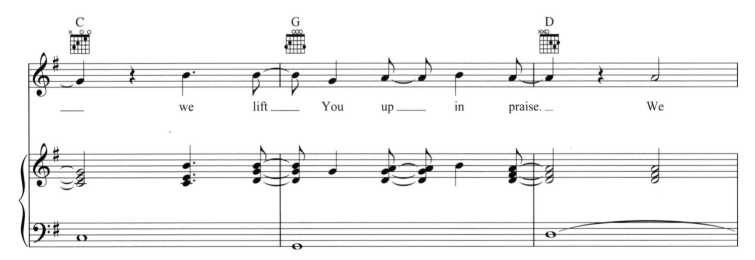

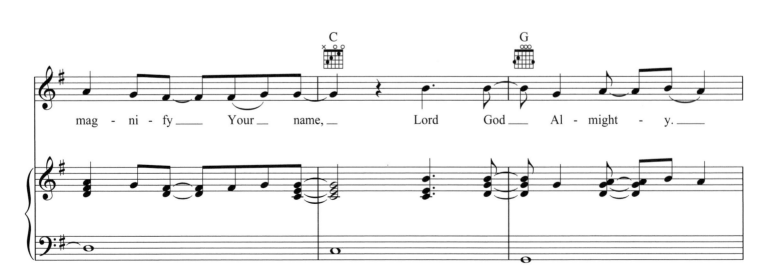

Your love__ fall,__ let it shine__ bright.) You__ a-lone__ de-serve the

hon-or and the glo-ry, You__ a-lone__ de-serve all our praise, so__

__ we wor-ship You__ and You__ a-lone.__

So__ we wor-ship You__ and You__ a-lone.__

THE ONE I LOVE

Words and Music by MAC POWELL,
TAI ANDERSON, MARK LEE and DAVID CARR

Oh, you __ of lit - tle faith, __ why do __ you let __ the wind __
Oh, you __ of lit - tle faith, __ oh, __ how quick - ly and

__ and the waves __ dis - tract __ you? __
how of - ten you have for - got - ten. __

Oh, you __ of lit - tle faith, __ don't __ you know __ that when __
Oh, you __ of lit - tle faith, __ aren't __ you tired __ of all __

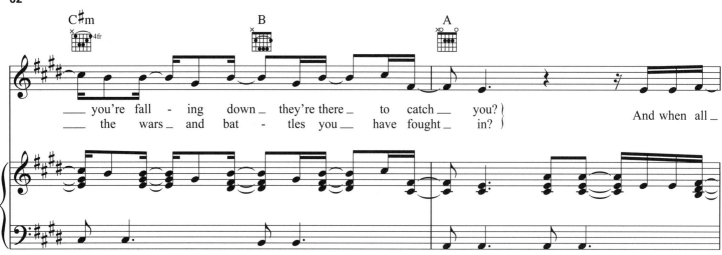

__ you're fall - ing down __ they're there __ to catch __ you? }
__ the wars __ and bat - tles you __ have fought __ in? }

And when all __

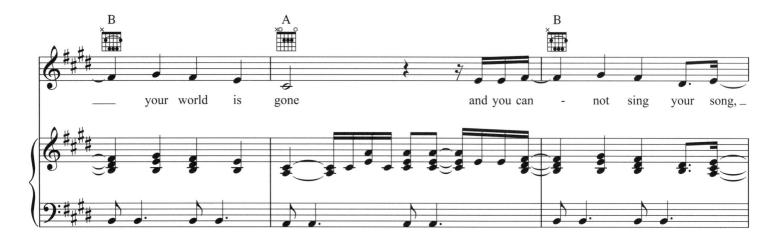

__ your world is gone

and you can - not sing your song, __

__

I will help __ you car - ry on, __ the __ one I __ love. __

the ___ one I ___ love. _____

Oh. _____

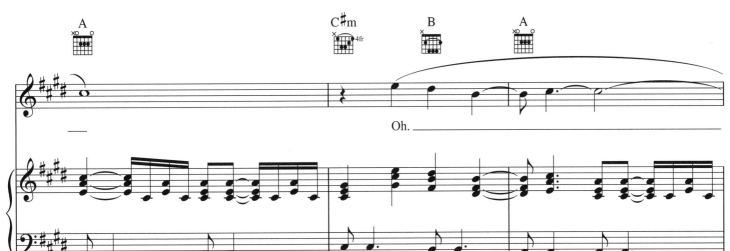

Oh. _____

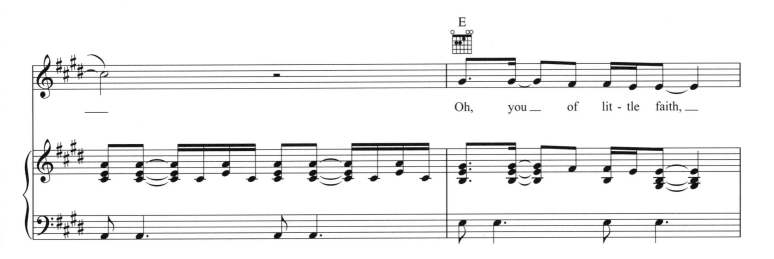

Oh, you ___ of lit-tle faith, ___

why do ___ you ___ let ___ the wind ___ and the waves ___ dis - tract ___

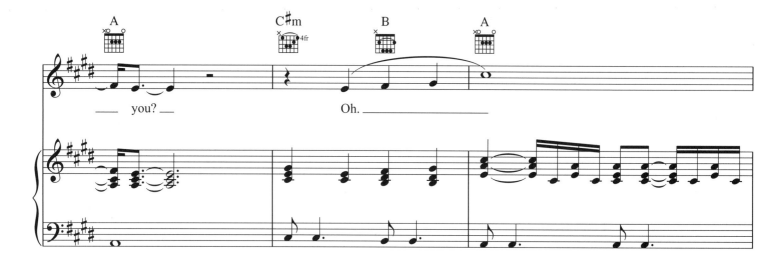

___ you? ___ Oh. _____

Oh. _____ Oh. _____